Pebble Plus

Pet Questions and Answers

PET FISH

Questions and Answers

by Christina Mia Gardeski

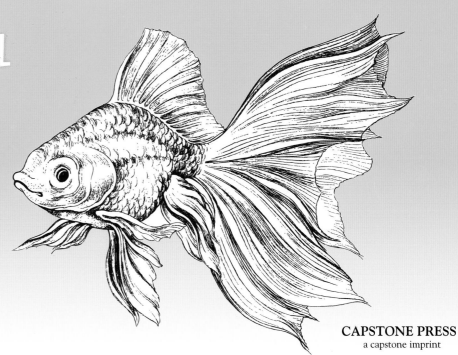

CAPSTONE PRESS
a capstone imprint

Pebble Plus is published by Capstone Press,
1710 Roe Crest Drive, North Mankato, Minnesota 56003
www.mycapstone.com

Library of Congress Cataloging-in-Publication Data
Names: Gardeski, Christina Mia, author.
Title: Pet fish : questions and answers / by Christina Mia Gardeski.
Description: North Mankato, Minnesota : Capstone Press, [2017] | Series: Pebble plus.
Pet questions and answers | Audience: Ages 4–8. | Audience: K to grade 3. | Includes
bibliographical references and index.
Identifiers: LCCN 2016007001 | ISBN 9781515703532 (library binding) |
ISBN 9781515703600 (pbk.) | ISBN 9781515703662 (ebook (pdf)
Subjects: LCSH: Aquarium fishes—Juvenile literature. | Children's questions and answers.
Classification: LCC SF457.25 .G37 2017 | DDC 639.34—dc23
LC record available at http://lccn.loc.gov/2016007001

Editorial Credits

Carrie Braulick Sheely and Michelle Hasselius, editors; Kayla Rossow, designer;
Pam Mitsakos, media researcher; Gene Bentdahl, production specialist

Photo Credits:

Alamy Images: roger askew, 21; Shutterstock: AndreJakubik, 5, carnival, 9, Moo teaforthree,
17, Nikiparonak, 1, 22, Nipon Laicharoenchokchai, 11, oksankash, 19, Pavel Vakhrushev, cover,
Photoman29, 13, S-F, 15, voylodyon, 7

Note to Parents and Teachers

The Pet Questions and Answers set supports national science standards related
to life science. This book describes and illustrates pet fish. The images support
early readers in understanding the text. The repetition of words and phrases
helps early readers learn new words. This book also introduces early readers
to subject-specific vocabulary words, which are defined in the Glossary section.
Early readers may need assistance to read some words and to use the Table
of Contents, Glossary, Read More, Internet Sites, Critical Thinking Using the
Common Core, and Index sections of the book.

Printed in China.
022016   007713

Table of Contents

Who Can Breathe Underwater?

My fish! Fish breathe through gills. Water carries gas called oxygen to the gills. The oxygen goes into the blood and through the fish's body. Fish need oxygen to live.

gill

How Do Fish Swim?

Fish wave their bodies back and forth to swim. Their tail fin pushes them through the water. Other fins help them turn or stop.

tail fin

Can Fish Smell?

Fish smell through two small holes on their heads. Water flows fast through these holes. It tells a fish if food or danger is near.

Do Fish Have Ears?

Fish do not have ears on the sides of their heads. They hear through inside ear parts. Fish have lines on their sides called cells. These cells help the fish know when something moves nearby.

What Do Fish Eat?

Fish eat fish flakes or frozen food

made from plants and animals.

Do not feed them too much!

This makes fish sick.

It also makes the water dirty.

Where Can I Keep My Fish?

Pet fish live in fish tanks
filled with water. A pump
keeps the water moving.
A filter keeps it clean.

Do Fish Sleep?

Fish do not sleep like people or other animals. They rest and save energy. Some fish settle down at the bottom of a tank. Others float in one spot.

Can I Train My Fish?

Most fish are smart.
They can be trained to do
simple tricks. Some fish swim
through hoops for treats.

Can I Pet My Fish?

Do not pet your fish. You might hurt it. Your hands can make the water dirty. Enjoy your fish from outside its home.

Glossary

energy—the strength to do active things without getting tired

filter—a machine that cleans liquids or gasses as they pass through it; a filter cleans the water in a fish tank

fin—a body part that fish use to swim and steer in water

flake—a small, thin piece of something

gill—a body part on the side of a fish; fish use their gills to breathe

oxygen—a colorless gas; humans and animals need oxygen to breathe

Read More

Ganeri, Anita. *Goldie's Guide to Caring for Your Goldfish.* Pet Guides. Chicago: Capstone Heinemann Library, 2013.

Graubart, Norman D. *My Fish.* Pets Are Awesome! New York: PowerKids Press, 2014.

Martin, Isabel. *Fish: A Question and Answer Book.* Animal Kingdom Questions and Answers. North Mankato, Minn.: Capstone Press, 2015.

Internet Sites

FactHound offers a safe, fun way to find Internet sites related to this book. All of the sites on FactHound have been researched by our staff.

Here's all you do:

Visit *www.facthound.com*

Type in this code: 9781515703532

Check out projects, games and lots more at
www.capstonekids.com

Critical Thinking
Using the Common Core

1. Explain how fish breathe. (Key Ideas and Details)

2. Fish tanks have filters. What are filters? (Craft and Structure)

3. How do fish rest? (Key Ideas and Details)

Index